Dedicated to my beautiful
children Josh & Nelly.

Special thank you to
my content advisors:

Jahnelle & Joshua Bryant,
Lawenda Telcide,
Brittany Pradere,
and Micah Guillet

Josh & Nelly's,
Promoting Reading Literacy

Copyright © 2021 by Joanne Telcide-Bryant

All rights reserved. No part of this publication may be reproduced, distributed, or transmitted in any form or by any means, including photocopying, recording, or other electronic or mechanical methods, without the prior written permission of the publisher, except in the case of brief quotations embodied in critical reviews and certain other noncommercial uses permitted by copyright law.

For permission requests, write to the author, addressed "Attention: Permissions " at joshnellys@outlook.com

First Edition:May 2021
Second Edition: June 2023

Josh & Nelly's Publishing
225 Main Street #234,
Hiram, GA, 30141

www.JoshNellysBooks.com

Ordering Information:
For details, contact
info@JoshNellysBooks.com

Print ISBN: 978-1-7370742-1-2
eBook ISBN: 978-1-7370742-0-5

Written By: Joanne Telcide-Bryant

Illustrated by: Travis A. Thompson

Josh & Nelly's Promoting Reading Literacy

Prologue:
Do you have a best friend? Can your pet be your best friend? What makes a puppy a best friend?

Read the reasons why this puppy is Nelly's best friend.

This story includes over 600 literacy words, a prologue, a glossary, and a set of comprehension questions.
Lexile Range: 210L - 400L

I love my puppy.

My puppy's name is

Coco is my best friend.

Coco reads books with me.

Coco sleeps with me.

Coco keeps the monsters away.

Coco helps me dress every morning.

Coco helps me eat.

Especially when I'm not hungry.

Coco takes bubble baths with me.

Coco helps me with my schoolwork.

Coco helps me clean my room.

Coco loves to have fun.
Coco gets her nails painted with me.
Coco plays dress-up with me.

Coco takes walks with me.

Coco runs with me.

Coco dances with me.

Coco is my special guest.

I love my puppy.
Coco is my best friend.

Best Friends Forever!

Glossary:
Dress-up: wear fancy clothes for fun
Especially: very much
Monster: a scary creature
Puppy: a baby dog between 1 and 2 years old
Special: one of a kind

Talk about what you have learned.
Who are the main story characters?
Where does Coco keep the monsters away?
What are some activities Coco likes to do with Nelly?
When does Coco get clean?
Why does Coco help Nelly eat?

What do you think?
Explain how having a best friend as a puppy can help you to feel better. What are some examples?